GROW IN
DIVINE
FAVOR

PATRICIA KING

Distributed by:

Patricia King Ministries

PO Box 1017

Maricopa AZ 85139

patriciaking.com

ISBN: 978-1-62166-511-3

Grow in Divine Favor

TABLE OF CONTENTS

FOREWORD

BY JOSHUA MILLS

Favor is one of the greatest discoveries you can make in this life. When you uncover its power and allow it to work in your life, something dramatic will happen for you. Throughout history we can see that those who had favor on their lives made the greatest impact on society and excelled in outstanding achievement. Some are born with it, while others learn how to tap into it and nurture it into abundance. But one thing is guaranteed… every world-changer will need to discover this power for themselves!

In my own life, favor has been the key that has opened countless opportunities for me to travel extensively all over the world, doing what I love to do most. I have been given the privileged opportunity to speak about miracles with both small and large audiences in more than sixty nations, and I am often asked the question, *"How do you receive all these invitations to travel to so many different places?"* Every time, my reply is the same: *"It must be favor."* Favor will take you where nothing else can.

Nothing remains the same once favor begins to work in and through you. The Holy Bible mentions favor almost 300 times, and we can read countless stories about this undeniable favor working in the lives of those who needed it more than anything else. Favor carried Joseph from the pit into the palace (see Genesis 39). David received favor and was able to release healing because of it (see 1 Samuel 16:22-23). The only way that the Israelites escaped from their torturous enslavement in Egypt was because of this influential favor.

In a moment, favor can change everything forever!

"The Lord caused the Egyptians to look favorably on the Israelites, and they gave the Israelites whatever they asked for" (Exodus 12:36 NLT).

Favor will open up hidden doors of access... it will allow you to revel in undue prosperity... it will connect you with your promises and bring you into a place of affluence.

Favor is supernatural. It will do things for you that you cannot do for yourself. Seek it, discern it, learn how to cooperate with it (see Proverbs 3:1-4).

Favor is unstoppable. It is like a mighty river that flows with unlimited potential. Once you discover this uncontainable force you will always have more than enough (see Job 10:12; Psalm 90:17).

Favor is bulletproof. It doesn't matter how strong the resistance appears, this force is invincible. When favor is on your side you become a force to be reckoned with (see Psalm 5:12; 23:4-6; 84:11)!

Favor is irresistible. It will bring people, opportunities, connections, miracles and finances into your lap (see Genesis 39:2-6; Ezra 7:6; Exodus 33:17; Psalm 89:17).

Favor is unbeatable. It contains the power for winning in life. Favor is better than riches – it is the golden key that unlocks the gates of immeasurable blessing for you (see Esther 5:2; Acts 7:9-10).

And favor is so much more…

I am so thankful that my dear friend Patricia King has written this important book about growing in divine favor. It is a jewel awaiting your discovery as Patricia unleashes this power for you! She is well qualified and extremely acquainted with this dimension of unmerited blessing and unusual grace. I have personally witnessed this divine favor upon her life and I believe that there is a supernatural transference for you within the pages of this book as you devour every word.

Prepare to receive sound wisdom and enlightenment. Prepare to receive practical insights that will change your life forever – prepare to *Grow in Divine Favor*!

—JOSHUA MILLS
International Conference Speaker
Bestselling Author of *31 Days to a Miracle Mindset*
Palm Springs, CA/Vancouver, BC
www.JoshuaMills.com

CHAPTER ONE

FAVOR DEFINED

FAVOR WILL

MAKE YOUR LIFE DELIGHTFUL

AND EXTREMELY FRUITFUL

FOR THE GLORY OF GOD.

WHAT IS FAVOR?

Passionately pursue favor! Why? Because favor is so extremely powerful. Favor will make your life delightful and extremely fruitful for the glory of God. The single blessing of God's undeserved, unmerited favor on your life will ensure success in all you do.

I remember years ago listening to a motivational speaker in a conference. Looking around the auditorium, I noticed that the attention of every person in attendance (including myself) was completely captured by the young man delivering the motivating message. He was definitely not endowed with a celebrity appearance; neither was he dressed in a wardrobe that would "wow" a crowd. Although he had a charming personality, his message was simple and contained principles that were common in motivational settings.

There was nothing uniquely profound about his insights, and his delivery was actually quite unpolished – yet I found myself hanging on every word. I had heard similar messages many times before, and probably the others in attendance had also.

After the meeting, I found myself in the crowd that was purchasing available materials at his resource table in the lobby. I loaded up with brochures, books, audio teachings, and manuals. Following my shopping spree, I went to the women's restroom and again heard numerous accolades regarding this young man's message.

What was it that made this man so desirable and successful? He was obviously saturated with *favor*!

Favor is a force – when it is in you and on you, you are blessed! Goodness and blessings are attracted to you like a magnet when you are filled with favor.

When I was a brand new Christian, I applied for a job that I was not trained for. Young in the Lord, I had read a book that taught that God's favor could open doors and opportunities for you. I believed it.

I proclaimed that God favored me and I would be chosen for the position. Over 100 people applied for the position, and many of them were much more qualified than I was – yet I was awarded the position. FAVOR!

What can favor look like in your life? The following are some examples.

You Are Favored When:

1. You are chosen for an employment position 100+ others applied for, even though you didn't have education, experience, or the qualifications needed.

2. You are in a long queue in the grocery store and a cashier whispers in your ear, "Come over to this check out lane," and opens it just for you.

3. You walk down the street and notice that many are smiling at you, wishing you a good day as you go by.

4. You share the gospel with a stranger in Starbucks after they invite you to sit down and drink your coffee with them. They lock in to everything you are saying and accept Christ.

5. You pray for a sick person that you meet at the bus stop. They are miraculously healed and brought to Christ, and then others ask you for prayer, too.

6. Your neighbors look for opportunities to come over and visit because they love your company.

7. Your relatives and friends want to move into your neighborhood to be near you.

8. You win the draw at work for the prize of a brand new car.

9. You check in for your flight and the attendant says, "I think I am going to upgrade you to first class."

10. You buy a new outfit and find that it went on sale for 70% off that very day.

11. Your newly published book flies off the shelf because it is so popular.

12. Your inbox is full of greetings from friends at Christmas time, birthdays and special occasions.

13. You have so many friends in your Facebook account that many are on the waiting list.

14. FedEx drops off gift boxes at your home and work addresses on a regular basis.

15. You are awarded "best employee" award at work.

16. You win many appeals and battles.

17. Everyone wants to be on your team.

18. Influenzas and viruses run through your region but you never get them.

19. Your prayers are being answered.

20. Your bank accounts are overflowing with more than what you need.

21. Your bills can be paid in full.

22. Your desires are getting fulfilled.

23. People are moved to bless you with gifts.

24. When you need help on a project, you have more volunteers than what you require.

25. Your children rise up to tell you how much they love and honor you.

26. Your spouse honors you in private and in public and is always thinking of ways to please you.

27. Effectual doors of opportunity are constantly opened to you.

28. You succeed in everything you put your hands to – all you do produces good fruit that remains.

29. When people rise up against you in judgment, it works together for your good instead of for your destruction.

30. You live in constant abundance and increase.

31. Goodness and mercy follow you all the days of your life, and blessings come upon you and overtake you.

32. You have assurance that all your sin is forgiven and your guilt and shame are removed.

33. You are aware that God is smiling at you.

34. You know that God celebrates you and doesn't just tolerate you.

35. On a mission trip, you go to an unreached village and everyone comes around you and accepts Christ!

WHEN YOU ARE FAVORED, YOU RECEIVE:

1. PRIVILEGE & PREFERENTIAL TREATMENT

2. BENEFITS & GIFTS

3. UNFAIR ADVANTAGE

FAVOR DEFINED[1]

1. TO BE APPROVED OF; TO BE LIKED

When divine favor is at work in your life, you have approval in the eyes of others. People like you. You might not understand why and perhaps they won't either. Sometimes you cannot explain the reason for the favor you receive – it's a gift. This is divine favor being activated in your life.

Like everyone else on the planet, I have experienced both rejection and favor – I like favor better – much better! And, so do you! It is wonderful to feel approval and to be liked.

On the day God created mankind, He said, "It is VERY good." He liked what He had made and He approved. That expectation for approval is built into you. That is why you do not handle rejection well. You were created for love and acceptance, and when people accept, like, and favor you, it feels good and right within.

We can never trust man's approval because individuals can be fickle, but God loves you, likes you,

---

[1] From YourDictionary.com and Merriam-Webster.com online dictionary.

approves of you, and favors you. There might be behavior that He does not approve of, but you are loved and favored in His sight. Dr. Brian Simmons once asked the following question in a seminar, "Do you know what God loves about you?" We all waited in anticipation for an answer. It was, "Everything!"

I was on a plane recently where the flight attendant kept staring and smiling at me. Every time I looked up, I found her looking at me. When she realized that I had caught her gaze, she smiled again. She gave me preferential treatment, and about halfway through the flight she came and asked me who I was and what I did for a living. I told her about our ministry and we shared some great exchanges throughout the remainder of the flight. At the end she said, "It was a pleasure meeting you – I really like you!" This is undeserved, unmerited favor.

I own businesses, one of which is a beauty salon in our community. It is a small beauty boutique with only three chairs, and it is in an older part of town. In the natural there is nothing that should attract people to it. However, from the time we received the vision for the business, we proclaimed the favor of God over it. Immediately after we opened the salon, we heard favorable comments from so many. The community adored our little beauty boutique, and through God-given favor the business flourished.

When the favor of God is present, individuals will approve of you and like you. The favor of God also rests on all that pertains to you – your family, your home, your businesses, your church, etc.

2. TO BE GIVEN PRIVILEGE AND PREFERENTIAL TREATMENT

When you are favored, you are granted privilege and special treatment. Joseph was favored in Potiphar's house, and although he was bought as a slave he lived like the master of the house. Later, when he was thrown into prison (due to the lies told by Potiphar's wife), he was not treated like a prisoner. The chief jailer gave him special treatment and privileges. Joseph was again favored.

I slipped into a meeting one time as a conference participant in order to enjoy the worship and the speaker's message. I took a seat toward the back because the meeting room was full, and I waited with anticipation for the service to begin. An usher identified me and invited me to take a seat up front. I was hesitant but he insisted, saying the head of the ministry had told him to bring me forward to sit with him, his wife, and his guest speaker. After the meeting they invited me into the green room for refreshments and fellowship. I was humbled by this act of favor shown me.

There have been times when the Lord has allowed me the privilege of sharing His love with dignitaries. It always amazes me when this favor is shown. One time my husband and I were invited to the Governor's Day Parade with Dr. Benson Idahosa in Benin City, Nigeria. We were escorted in a limousine to the event that hosted over one hundred thousand participants. We sat in the governor's booth, were filmed for the national television news broadcast, and were invited to prophesy over leaders following the parade. We were virtually unknown, but because of our association with Dr. Benson Idahosa we received undeserved, unmerited favor.

3. TO BE GIVEN BENEFITS AND GIFTS

God's favor opens realms for benefits and gifts to be given you. Why did the wise men bring gifts to Jesus? Why did they not report back to Herod? It was because they favored Jesus. They had heard about Christ's birth and went to find Him. Jesus had not done anything yet to deserve the extravagant gifts they brought, as He was just a baby. The wise men were not related to Him and were not personal friends of the family, yet Jesus was favored by the wise men.

I have been deeply touched by this aspect of the favor of God. Often when I am out on the road serving the Lord, individuals will bless me with a personal gift. These acts of kindness deeply touch my heart, as I know that most of them have never met me before. My heart is to simply be a blessing to those I serve and I am not expecting gifts or recompense in return, but sometimes I am literally overwhelmed by these kind gestures. One night back in my hotel room, I was weeping as I read through the kind and encouraging notes and opened the gifts. I said, "God, I am so undeserving of all this." I could feel Him smile and say, "That's right – it is undeserved, unmerited favor. It is divine favor."

4. TO BE GIVEN UNFAIR ADVANTAGE

When you are favored, you have advantage that you never earned or deserved. We took a team to Tijuana, Mexico, to plant an outreach center in 1985. We had very little money and no accommodations had been secured before we left. When we arrived, we discovered that there were eighteen-month to two-year waiting periods for housing. We prayed and sought the Lord for three days. On the third evening, some of our team members went to the laundromat to wash their clothes, and they took their guitars. While waiting for their laundry to finish the cycle, they sang praise songs and a crowd gathered – including the owner of the laundromat. He was a Christian and asked them what they were doing in Tijuana. They shared our vision and the fact that we did not have a place to live. He said, "Well, I am a landlord and I happen to have a large four-bedroom house that is available right now." He further explained, however, that there was a problem because another family was on the waiting list and they had been waiting for over eighteen months for it to open up. He said that he would give us the house if the other family decided not to take it.

We went back and prayed, and within 24 hours we received a call saying the family who was going to take the building was suddenly that day blessed with an offer of a job in another city. They cancelled their name from the waiting list and we acquired the house. There were many Mexican friends we met later who were perplexed when we told them how quickly we secured our place. We were able to easily get three more plac-es in the next year as our ministry grew. God's favor toward us gave the advantage.

I once had an individual who wanted me to partner with them in an investment. The extravagant advantage they were giving me was unwarranted. When I asked why they would want to do that, they said, "Because, you have so much favor on your life that if you partner with me on this, I know the endeavor will do well. The favor God has given you will give us advantage in this market." As a result, I was blessed with a partnership in the endeavor.

LET'S REVIEW THE DEFINITIONS OF FAVOR:

1. To be approved of; to be liked

2. To be given privilege and preferential treatment

3. To be given benefits and gifts

4. To be given unfair advantage

Take a moment to dream. What would your life look like if you lived all the time in the fulfillment of all the definitions of favor listed above? Is that something you would like? The truth is, this is exactly what God had planned when He created you. He never intended mankind to suffered rejection. He created you to be favored and to enjoy the benefits of such favor.

CHAPTER TWO

GOD'S FAVOR &
THE COVENANT

IF YOU LOVE JESUS...

THE FAVOR OF GOD IS AVAILABLE TO YOU 24/7.

YOU ARE AN HEIR OF HIS DIVINE FAVOR

FAVOR FOR A LIFETIME

You can experience favor every day of your life. The Scripture declares, "His favor is for a lifetime" (Psalm 30:5). That means it doesn't grow weak over time and it isn't missing one day and present on another. The favor that God gives you is available every day of your life.

Divine favor is His gift to you, and it is the purest and most powerful form of favor in the universe. You cannot earn it, you do not deserve it – it is a gift you receive within when you accept Jesus Christ as your Lord and Savior.

It is possible for individuals to earn natural favor with others when they are gifted or talented, successful in a career or project, financially prosperous, physically attractive, or if they have a winning personality. But God's divine undeserved, unmerited favor trumps it all. If you love Jesus, the favor of God is available to you 24/7. You are an heir of divine favor.

Jesus grew in favor with God and men (see Luke 2:52). Jesus is fully favored by the Father for all eternity and He has given His favor to you – for free! Like Jesus, you can grow in favor with both God and others. Two thousand years ago, Jesus died on the cross to establish an eternal, unbreakable covenant between God and man. In this covenant is the promise of undeserved, unmerited favor for all who believe. Let's examine this covenant.

THE COVENANT OF BLESSING

A covenant is a legally binding agreement between two or more people or two or more parties of people. We see covenants today in marriage, business partnerships, contracts, house purchases, etc.

The Bible is a legal document that outlines and describes the old covenant (or contract) and the new covenant (or contract) between God and man.

COVENANTS REQUIRE:

1. **Clear description of terms and benefits.**

   Using a business contract as an example, it is important that each party knows what the terms of the contract and the benefits are. Due to the fact that once contracts are signed they are legally binding, it is important to draw up the terms carefully. A marriage covenant is similar in that it is a legally binding agreement.

2. Agreement to the terms and benefits by the parties involved.

All parties involved are to mutually agree to the terms and benefits.

3. Signing the covenant.

Covenants must have the signatures of the parties and witnesses involved.

4. Keeping the terms of the covenant.

In order for a covenant to remain fulfilled, the terms must be kept. In a marriage covenant, for example, we vow to be faithful to our spouse. If one of the parties engages in infidelity, then the covenant is breached and it is legal reason for divorce (or terminating the covenant).

God desired relationship with man, but man sinned and broke the perfect union he originally shared with

God. As a result, it was impossible for man to be reconciled to God on his own merit or through his own efforts. With sin now in his system and DNA, he could not be in union with a holy God but was, in fact, separated from Him. God determined, planned, and implemented a glorious restoration of the relationship through the establishment of an eternal, unbreakable, covenant of blessing.

- **The covenant was between God and man.**

- **God would set the terms and benefits.**

- **God and man would agree to the terms and benefits.**

- **The covenant would be signed/sealed in blood.**

- **God and man would keep the terms for eternity.**

Due to the fact that man was unable to keep the terms, God became Man. Jesus is fully God and He is also fully Man because He became Man. As God and as Man, Jesus made a covenant with Himself that could never be broken. He, Himself, as both God and Man, took full responsibility to fulfill all the terms of the covenant for all time and to give freely all the benefits to those who receive Him.

The covenant was signed in blood through His death on the cross and witnessed. The Bible says that there are three that bear witness: the Spirit, the water (the Word), and the blood (the covenant) (1 John 5:7-8).

THE BENEFITS OF THE COVENANT:

Let's further examine this glorious covenant.

1. **CHRIST WOULD FULFILL ALL THE TERMS OF THE COVENANT FOR MANKIND.**

   On your behalf (and on behalf of all mankind), Christ fulfilled all the terms for you. He did what you would never be able to do for yourself.

2. **BLESSINGS WOULD COME UPON THOSE WHO ENTER THE NEW COVENANT AND OVERTAKE THEM (DEUTERONOMY 28:1-2).**

   The definition of *blessing* is "**to invoke <u>favor</u> upon and to empower to prosper.**" When you accept Christ into your heart as your Savior and Lord, you enter the new covenant – a covenant of blessing. You cannot earn any of the blessings. They are a gift to you as a partaker of the new covenant.

3. **EVERY CURSE THAT CAME AS A CONSEQUENCE OF SIN, DEATH, AND THE LAW, IS ANNIHILATED.**

When you are in covenant with God, you have been redeemed from the curse that came as a result of sin, death, and the Law. Christ became a curse for you, and in exchange He gave you all the blessings (see Galatians 3:13-14).

4. **EVERY PROMISE IN THE WORD BELONGS TO THOSE IN COVENANT (EPHESIANS 1:3; 2 PETER 1:2-4).**

With all the curses removed, the blessings remain for you in fullness. When you receive all the promises of God's blessings for you, you partake of His divine nature.

5. **THOSE IN COVENANT RELATIONSHIP WITH GOD THROUGH CHRIST ARE RIGHTEOUS BEFORE GOD (2 CORINTHIANS 5:21).**

You are completely righteous before God through Christ Jesus. You are favored in the sight of God because you received His Son.

CHRIST'S PART:

- To fulfill and keep all the terms of the covenant for all eternity.

- To freely give all the benefits to those who believe.

OUR PART:

- To believe in Jesus Christ as Savior and Lord.

- To receive Jesus Christ into our life as Savior and Lord.

- To live in the blessings of the covenant by faith.

   For by grace you have been saved through faith; and that not of yourselves, it is the gift of God; not as a result of works, so that no one may boast. – **Ephesians 2:8-9**

GRACE AND FAVOR ARE TWINS

When you read Scriptures on grace you can often replace it with the word *favor*. *Grace* means: undeserved, unmerited **favor** and God's divine influence upon the heart.

Verses that contains the word *grace* can often be exchanged to mean God's *favor* toward you.

SCRIPTURES
ON GRACE AND FAVOR

Exodus 12:36

And the Lord had given the people favor ... Thus they plundered the Egyptians.

2 Samuel 15:25

If I find favor in the sight of the Lord, then He will ... show me ... His habitation.

Psalm 30:5

His favor is for a lifetime.

Psalm 30:7

O Lord, by Your favor You have made my mountain to stand strong. [Note: your "mountain" can be your mountain of influence.]

Psalm 84:11

The Lord gives grace and glory; No good thing does He withhold from those who walk uprightly.

Psalm 90:17

Let the favor of the Lord our God be upon us; and confirm for us the work of our hands; yes, confirm the work of our hands.

Proverbs 8:35

For he who finds me (Wisdom) finds life and obtains favor from the Lord.

Proverbs 16:15

In the light of a king's face is life, and his favor is like a cloud with the spring rain.

Luke 4:19 (NLT)

The time of the Lord's favor has come.

Acts 15:11

We are saved through the grace [special favor] of the Lord Jesus.

Acts 20:32

And now I commend you to God and to the word of His grace, which is able to build you up and to give you the inheritance among all those who are sanctified.

Romans 5:2

We have obtained our introduction by faith into this grace in which we stand.

Romans 6:14

For sin shall not be master over you, for you are not under law but under grace.

2 Corinthians 9:8

God is able to make all grace abound to you, so that always having all sufficiency in everything, you may have an abundance for every good deed.

2 Corinthians 12:9 (NLT)

My grace is all you need.

2 Timothy 1:9

Who has saved us and called us with a holy calling, not according to our works, but according to His own purpose and grace which was granted us in Christ Jesus from all eternity.

Titus 2:11; 3:7

For the grace of God has appeared, bringing salvation to all men ... Being justified by His grace we would be made heirs according to the hope of eternal life.

Hebrews 4:16

Let us draw near with confidence to the throne of grace, so that we may receive mercy and find grace.

Hebrews 13:9

Your strength comes from God's grace (NLT).

1 Peter 1:2

May grace and peace be yours in the fullest measure.

GLEANING UNDERSTANDING
OF GOD'S FAVOR
THROUGH ABRAHAM'S LIFE

The very first thing God spoke over man was a blessing: "God blessed them" (Genesis 1:28).

Remember that *blessing* means "to invoke favor upon and to empower to prosper." When you read the word *blessing* in the Bible, you can remember that. God has always been a God of blessing. You were created for blessing: to be favored and empowered to prosper!

When God introduced Himself to Abraham, He declared: "I will bless you, and make your name great; And so you shall be a blessing ... and in you all the families of the earth will be blessed" (Genesis 12:2-3).

Abraham believed that God would favor him and empower him to prosper as he followed Him, and it was accounted to him as righteousness. With Sarah, Abraham left the land of the Chaldeans expecting to be favored, blessed, and prospered by the God who had promised him these things.

All the days of Abraham's life he was highly favored and blessed – even his mistakes were taken care of by God. He was blessed with a wonderful relationship with God, angelic visitations, a great marriage, children, land acquisitions, flocks, herds, gold, silver, servants, and even his own army.

Abraham was highly favored all through his life because he believed in the covenant of blessing God had established with him (see Genesis 15).

Abraham expected favor to manifest – God had promised! Abraham believed all that God promised and received the blessing. He never doubted. This is so simple.

In Galatians 3:13-14, we read:

> Christ redeemed us from the curse of the Law, having become a curse for us – for it is written, "Cursed is everyone who hangs on a tree" – in order that in Christ Jesus the blessing of Abraham might come to the Gentiles, so that we would receive the promise of the Spirit through faith.

The covenant of Abraham was for all his descendants. Isaac understood this and lived in the blessing.

Jacob understood this and lived in the blessing. Joseph understood this and lived in the blessing. All of them lived in favor because of the covenant God made with Abraham. This blessing is for all who believe.

Unfortunately, after Joseph passed, the children of Israel forgot their covenant and they allowed themselves to be oppressed. They forgot who they were. They were highly blessed and favored by God but they failed to remember and believe.

When God heard their groanings, He sent a deliverer. He was being faithful to His covenant with Abraham and was blessing the descendants.

Sadly, as we follow the children of Israel through the wilderness we see that they doubted the goodness of God. Even though they had an active covenant of blessing through Abraham and although God had blessed them with their own tremendous promise for safe passage to their own land, they doubted Him. As a result, they never entered their blessing.

Like Abraham, Isaac, Jacob, and Joseph, they could have lived in extravagant undeserved, unmerited, favor and blessing, but they failed to believe that God was good and that He intended to bless them all their days according to His covenant.

You have an eternal, unbreakable, covenant through Christ. All the blessings are yours! His favor is yours. This glorious covenant of grace is divine favor.

CHAPTER THREE

PRINCIPLES FOR GROWING IN FAVOR

PART ONE

THE TRUTH IS...

YOU ARE FAVORED, LOVED, AND BLESSED

IN CHRIST BEYOND MEASURE.

The Importance of Faith

In the previous chapter, we saw the difference in results between Abraham who believed in the goodness, blessing, and favor of God and the Israelites as they went through the desert with hardened hearts of unbelief.

Abraham's life was blessed and favored all of his days when he followed God out of the land of the Chaldeans, but the generation of Hebrews who departed from Egypt to follow Him into the Promised Land lived with discouragement, fear, and negativity. Even though they had blessing all around them, they could not see it, and they refused to believe.

Abraham had faith but the Israelites did not. Abraham was promised blessing if he followed God, and the Israelites were given the same promise – it was the same covenant. Abraham lived in the full manifestation of the blessing of the covenant and the Israelites did not. Faith made the difference.

Now faith is the substance of things hoped for, the evidence of things not seen. – **Hebrews 11:1 (KJV)**

The Scripture states that faith is the substance of hope. Hope is a joyful expectation. It is good to hope, but it is faith that secures the promises. Faith is when what you believe becomes an internal reality. For example, I have faith that Jesus is Lord, and that He has given me eternal life. This is not something I am merely joyfully expecting; this is an internal reality. Hope looks at the future, but faith receives the future into the "now."

Hebrews 11:1 also teaches that faith is the evidence of what you cannot see. I cannot see Jesus living within me with my natural eye. I cannot see eternal life, but I believe. My faith is the evidence.

The day after I was born again, I shared the gospel the best I could with some friends of mine who were steeped in the New Age. They were hard on me and had a difficult time understanding that I believed what they perceived was "nonsense." "How can you believe that?" they asked. I responded by saying, "The Bible says it." They laughed and ignorantly challenged me, saying, "Man wrote the Bible – anyone can make up a story." I was a brand new babe in Christ and did not have training on how to respond, but I replied with absolute conviction, "I just KNOW." My faith was the evidence for me. I had that huge witness within me that my search for life's answers was over. Jesus was all I needed and He was the end of my search. I KNEW IT! My faith was the evidence. That is the difference between faith and hope. Hope is the joyful expectation, but when you are in faith, you KNOW what you believe is true to the very core of your being. You have it! You possess it! It is your internal reality and it is based on the truth of God's Word.

Truth Versus Fact

Two realms (dimensions) that surround us are the natural realm of time and the eternal realm. Facts are of the realm of time and truth is of the eternal realm. Your faith is the connector that brings the truth from the eternal realm into the time realm.

Truth is based on the promises of God's Word.

Ephesians 1:3 says, "Blessed be the God and Father of our Lord Jesus Christ, who has blessed us with every spiritual blessing in the heavenly places in Christ."

Second Peter 1:2-4 says, "Grace and peace be multiplied to you in the knowledge of God and of Jesus our Lord; seeing that His divine power has granted to us everything pertaining to life and godliness, through the true knowledge of Him who called us by His own glory and excellence. For by these He has granted to us His precious and magnificent promises, so that by them you may become partakers of the divine nature, having escaped the corruption that is in the world by lust."

The Scripture makes it clear that we have been granted every promise and blessing in God. These were given (past tense) two thousand years ago when Jesus sealed the covenant between God and man with His own blood. Amazing!

The fact (a situational reality in the realm of time) might be that you suffer rejection, but the truth (the eternal reality) is that you are favored, loved, and blessed in Christ beyond measure.

It is wise to acknowledge a fact but not to respond to it as though it were truth. Acknowledging a fact will help reveal what promise is needed to overcome a problem or grow and increase with blessing in any given situation.

For example, Jonathan, a young entrepreneur, submitted his new product to three corporations that he wholeheartedly believed would be interested in becoming significant clients. One of them turned him down for an interview and the other two rejected his product.

The fact was, his attempts failed and were rejected. Jonathan understood that facts are only facts, and he had chosen to live in the truth. He knew the Bible said that Christ would cause him to triumph in all things, that everything he put his hands to would prosper, and that he was growing in favor with God and man.

He went into prayer and received some wisdom from God on how to proceed, as well as some promises from the Word that ensured his success. He proceeded to receive some good critiques on his product that helped him perfect it, and he also received some input on perfecting his presentation. All the while, he pressed in for the favor that was promised him in the Scriptures.

Jonathan proceeded in faith, believing he was blessed, filled with favor, and empowered to succeed. He stood on the promises in the Word. Over the next months as he focused on his goal, he pursued three more clients and asked the previous three rejections for another opportunity to present. Out of the six proposals, four of them made commitments and the other two said they might be interested later.

Jonathan BELIEVED he would succeed. He had hope (joyful expectation) and active faith that God's favor and blessing would go with him and grant him great results. The results proved it.

Hebrews 11:6

And without faith it is impossible to please Him, for he who comes to God must believe that He is and that He is a rewarder of those who seek Him.

Mark 9:23

All things are possible to him who believes.

James 1:8 (KJV)

A double minded man is unstable in all his ways.

Mark 11:24

All things for which you pray and ask, believe that you have received them, and they will be granted you.

Romans 1:17

The righteous man shall live by faith.

1 Timothy 6:12

Fight the good fight of faith. [Note: fight rejection, unworthiness, etc.]

1 John 5:4

This is the victory that has overcome the world – our faith.

CORE BELIEFS

You are what you believe in your core!

In the world of health and fitness, instructors will encourage those they train and coach to develop their physical core. It is equally important to have a strong core within your soul by building and maintaining healthy core beliefs and values. Everything in your life flows from your established beliefs within.

The Bible teaches us the truth and this is what we are to believe. Jesus said, "ONLY BELIEVE" (Mark 5:36).

1 John 5:7-8

There are three that testify: the Spirit and the water (Word) and the blood (covenant).

These three bear witness to the truth – they will not bear witness to a lie.

Learn to identify the lies that stand in the way of your favor and replace them with truth. Every time the truth is challenged, stand firm. Eventually the truth will become your default.

You are favored by God and are blessed beyond measure. Do you believe this when circumstances seem to contradict the promise of God's Word? Continue to meditate on the promises concerning favor; choose to believe them even in the midst of crisis, until they become part of the fabric of your core beliefs. All your core beliefs (your default beliefs) are to be based on what God says about you and not what circumstances or the enemy's lies attempt to dictate.

When you establish core beliefs regarding the favor of God in your life, then that favor will attract more favor. It becomes a realm and atmosphere around you.

People who believe they are rejected have a realm of rejection around them that attracts more rejection. Their core beliefs create that atmosphere. Again, you can create the realm of favor by establishing God's promises concerning His favor within your heart.

YOUR CHOICE:

- Believe the truth and you will be blessed and highly favored.

- Believe the lie and you will fall short of the promise and will suffer the consequences of what you believe.

Meditate on the favor of God until you believe it.

RESISTANCE TRAINING

In the field of sports, the athlete gains strength through resistance. It is the same in the spirit realm. The moment you choose to stand on God's promise of favor toward you, you might find circumstances that will cause you to doubt. When you cast down the doubt and cleave to the promise, you will be strengthened in your core beliefs.

You eventually will drive out of your soul anything that is contrary to the truth. Your core will be unshakable in your belief in God's favor. Actively establish your core belief and resist every thought or circumstance that speaks contrary to the promises of God. You are favored! That favor lasts for a lifetime! That favor is a gift! It is yours!

Only believe!

PRINCIPLE TWO:

THE POWER OF WORDS

James teaches us in James 3:2 that if we do not stumble in what we say, we are a perfect man and able to bridle the whole body. He further expounds in verse six that our entire life and its course is affected by the words we speak. Words bring death or life; blessing or cursing (see James 3:10).

Many have cursed themselves with rejection and failure rather than with favor and success simply by speaking curses over their own lives. I have heard individuals say, "I am always left out," or "I am constantly rejected." The more you make statements that are contrary to the truth of God's Word, the more you set yourself up for a curse. The words you speak will curse you or bless you, so watch very carefully over the words that proceed from your mouth.

Jesus described the power of His words to His disciples in John 6:63 when He said, "The words I have spoken to you are spirit and are life." Like Jesus, speak words that will create life and blessing.

I love to intentionally make decrees of God's favor over my life. A "God-decree" is a holy proclamation that carries the authority of our King.

Job 22:28: "Decree a thing and it will be established."

Esther 8:8 says that a decree made in the name of a king may not be revoked.

In the Old Testament, God had the priests speak words of blessing and favor over the children of Israel. This Aaronic blessing remains a perpetual decree that can also be proclaimed by God's New Testament priesthood. You can proclaim this over your own life:

Numbers 6:22-27

Then the Lord spoke to Moses, saying,

"Speak to Aaron and to his sons, saying, 'Thus you shall bless the sons of Israel. You shall say to them:

The Lord bless you, and keep you;

The Lord make His face shine on you,

And be gracious to you;

The Lord lift up His countenance on you,

And give you peace.'

So they shall invoke My name on the sons of Israel, and I then will bless them."

What God was saying was that if this decree was made over the children of Israel, then He would bless them. His blessing was made manifest through the power of the words spoken.

Your words have power. Have you been blessing yourself? Or…?

It helps sometimes to identify and make a list of negative words that you or others have spoken over you that have hindered your growth in God's favor.

As you identify words that have served as curses, do not be overwhelmed. God is about to set you free.

Isaiah 54:17

No weapon that is formed against you will prosper; and every tongue that accuses you in judgment you will condemn. This is the heritage of the servants of the Lord.

Forgive yourself and anyone who has cursed you with negative words. Bless those who have cursed you and then command every negative word to become powerless and without effect.

Now replace with words of blessing. Create decree statements that bless your life with favor, and speak them out.

PRINCIPLE THREE:

DEVELOP THE CHARACTER AND NATURE OF GOD IN YOUR LIFE

Every aspect of God's nature attracts favor. For example, one of the aspects of His nature is kindness. People who are kind are favored. Generosity is another aspect of His nature. Generous people are favored. Every time you manifest His nature, it attracts favor.

On the other hand, characteristics that are contrary to His nature attract rejection. If you are being rejected, examine yourself to see if there are ungodly characteristics that you are manifesting. For example, God is patient. Those who are constantly impatient are not usually favored and are oftentimes critically judged by others. God is slow to anger. Those who have a short fuse are not usually favored. Many are afraid of such people and feel like they are walking on thin ice around them.

WHERE THERE IS SMOKE THERE IS FIRE!

I have met many people who are absolutely wonderful yet seem to hit pockets of rejection and resistance constantly. When this happens to you, humble yourself and ask those who are rejecting or resisting you if they would mind sharing honestly the things in you that seem to create that response.

When people do share, make sure you do not get defensive. If a number of people are saying the same thing, then you might need to look at it and make some changes. It won't do you any good to continue in the same things that are creating the reactions. That will just give you more of the same. When it is a pattern, you need to learn from it and make adjustments.

Cultivate a life filled with the attributes of God. Those attributes live within your born-again nature[2] and by faith you can release them to fill your soul and manifest in your life.

----

[2] To be born again is to receive Christ's life and nature within you by faith. When you ask Jesus to forgive you of your sins and invite Him to be your Lord and Savior, He comes into your heart and makes you a brand new creation. This is called the born-again experience. Simply pray and ask. He will come in and grant you the gift of eternal life! "For God so loved the world, that He gave His only begotten Son, that whoever believes in Him shall not perish, but have eternal life" (John 3:16).

It is helpful to make a list of the godly attributes that you already possess and note the favor that accompanies those particular attributes. Invite the Lord to help you expand and grow in new attributes that perhaps are not developed yet.

In the same manner, ask the Holy Spirit to reveal to you any ungodly attributes or behaviors that attract resistance and rejection in your life. Once you identify these, you can ask the Lord to forgive you. First John 1:9 says that when you confess your sin, He is faithful and just to forgive you and to cleanse you from all unrighteousness. Then proceed to ask for the Lord's grace in order to replace the ungodly with godly attributes.

PRINCIPLE FOUR:

DEVELOP YOUR GIFTS, TALENTS, AND ABILITIES

God has given everyone special motivations and gifts. These gifts as they are developed attract favor and open doors for you (see Proverbs 18:16).

I have a friend who is a talented musician, song-writer, and worship leader. He is very favored due to his gift, and he has many invitations to minister. Other friends are talented in the prophetic, in humor, in sports and art, in business discernment, and in public speaking. All of them are favored because of the gifts they have developed.

You are unique and you can develop gifts, talents and skills. Your developed gifts, talents, and abilities will open doors of favor for you.

You might want to take time to make a list of your gifts, talents, and abilities, celebrating the Lord with each one as you thank Him for them. Invite His favor to fill them more and more as you look for ways to develop them further.

PRINCIPLE FIVE:
YOUR OUTWARD APPEARANCE MATTERS

First impressions are extremely important. God does not look at the outward appearance but He looks at the heart (see 1 Samuel 16:7). However, most people will assess others on the basis of their first impression of outward appearance and presentation. Once that impression is established in the mind, it is hard to change it.

Your outward appearance and presentation are what people notice first before they ever get to know the "inner you." If someone at first rejects the outward appearance, they might possibly never get to know the inner you. If they favor the outward appearance at the time of their first impression, they will probably want to get to know you better.

Remember: Jesus grew in favor with both God and man. We are not to be "men-pleasers" in that we compromise our morals, beliefs, convictions, or values in order to win the favor of others. Absolutely not!

You must always be true to God and to yourself in your core. And yet it is important to understand the dynamics of outward appearance and how it relates to divine favor.

The development of both outer and inner beauty is important. Favor or lack of favor in the eyes of man is usually initially established at the first meeting. That means it is very important.

Imagine four people standing in a lineup, and you have to pick the one you most favor. You have never met them before and you have no resumé or bio that describes their gifts, talents, and abilities. They have not spoken to you, so you do not know their perspectives on life, principles, or values. You have to choose the one you most favor based on physical appearance alone.

Here are the descriptions of the four people.

(For the sake of this exercise,
these four people are women in their fifties):

PERSON #1 – DISHEVELED

Wrinkled clothes

Scuffed shoes

Bushy eyebrows – not plucked

Teeth – coffee stained, need maintenance and dental care

Hair – untrimmed, unfashionable, no luster

Face, skin, and lips – pale, dull, and toxic, without healthy natural color

Eyes – looking at floor

Sad countenance, seems to be insecure

Overweight

PERSON #2 – OLD FASHIONED/NO FASHION

Hair tightly pulled back into bun on top of her head

Shoe style from the fifties – penny loafers

Ankle socks

Unshaved legs

Long black skirt to mid-calf

Frumpy turtleneck top

Bulky cardigan

Two disturbing large fat-cell growths on eyelids

Average weight

Skin looks healthy – (no makeup)

Lips are naturally pink – (no makeup)

Teeth are healthy and well maintained – a bit yellowed due to age

Serious countenance – frown lines

PERSON #3 – OVERDONE

Over-tanned from tanning booth or chemical tanning

Big hair – over-bleached

Caked-on foundation, makeup, and powder

Predominant false eyelashes with tons of mascara

Bright lipstick with liner that goes way beyond the natural lip line

Tons of "bling"

Fishnet stockings and five-inch heels

Exaggerated smile (like a pose)

Body movements and countenance are obviously saying, "Look at me – pick ME!"

Clean, tidy

White teeth (maybe too much whitening)

A little overweight but still of a healthy weight

PERSON #4 – WELL DONE

Natural complexion with tastefully applied foundation, makeup and powder (not excessive)

Eyes with gentle and fashionable makeup application

Fashionable clothes but not overdone

Fashionable and feminine shoe wear

Fashionable hairstyle that frames the face well

Fashionable jewelry to accent clothes

Neat and tidy, well groomed

Teeth are white and well maintained

Countenance is bright, exudes optimism

Stands with appearance that comes from restful internal confidence

Based solely on outward appearance, which one would you most favor and why?

___ Person #1   ___ Person #2   ___ Person #3   ___ Person #4

_____

_____

_____

If two people apply for the same job with identical qualifications and experience, the outward appearance and the way they present themselves to people will probably be the clincher points for who gets the position.

Everyone is beautiful! God says that you are fearfully and wonderfully made (Psalm 139:14). Highlight that beautiful you! Cultivate the heart beauty before anything else, but the outward appearance does really matter, too.

I love helping women who desire to marry find their mate – I really love it! I always let them know that their outward appearance matters. That is a man's first impression. He must fall in love with the heart, but if he can't see the heart due to the outward mess, you will likely have trouble connecting.

When you favor yourself from within, you will spend more attention on the outward appearance (including fresh breath, dental care, and deodorized underarms, too). Don't be afraid to go for a makeover if needed. Someone that can be more objective might really be able to help you. Be open to input and to change (and men – this goes for you, too)!

Don't be afraid to ask the "opinions" of others. Often we get locked into a view of ourselves that is quite different from how others see us. Try asking friends that you trust to give you an evaluation, and explain to them that you want an HONEST evaluation[3] without holding back.

Oh, and by the way: don't allow any negative feedback to create rejection in you. Remember that you are favored. You are awesome! The feedback will help you. You might not be in agreement with it all, but it is worth reviewing. Humbly regard the input – faithful are the wounds of a friend!

---

[3] In the Appendix, an evaluation covering various catagories is included, which you can give to your friends to fill out on your behalf.

CHAPTER FOUR

PRINCIPLES FOR GROWING IN FAVOR

PART TWO

YOU RECEIVE WHAT YOU EXPECT.

BE FAVOR MINDED! EXPECT FAVOR! LOOK FOR FAVOR!

Expect Favor

I f you expect rejection and resistance, you will most often get it. You usually receive what you are expecting. Be favor minded! Expect favor! Look for favor!

I believe in intentionality. Purposely and intentionally expect favor.

Before I go on a flight, I stir up an expectation for favor. I get excited about a possible upgrade, a good seat, an opportunity to witness, or some great downloads from the Lord during the flight. There is something so powerful about an optimistic, expectation for something good to happen.

I am not saying that every time I go to the airport with an expectation to get an upgrade to business class I get it. But the optimistic expectation provides a realm of good things – if it is not in the upgrade it is in something else. I am always looking with expectation for favor.

You will be tested on your attitude when your expectation fails, too. I have found that a heart of thanksgiving rather than grumbling will always provide breakthrough. Sometimes little children when disappointed get a bit pouty and cry over what they didn't get to do or have when they expected it. We are not to respond like that; we are to be mature.

Remain thankful, happy and expectant, even when something doesn't work out the way you desired it. When you cultivate expectancy in your life, things that you haven't even believed for come to you at the most surprising times.

Constantly stir up expectation and look for even the slightest breakthrough – then celebrate it. When the favor comes, even in a small measure, declare, "That is the favor of God!" and then… keep looking for more.

Before engaging in street evangelism, I like to pray for favor and invite expectation for it to fill my heart. After preparing, I expect favor on the streets. If you do not have favor from God when you go to reach the lost, they will not listen to the gospel. You need favor. Expect it. If you go for a job interview or even something as mundane as grocery shopping, stir up an expectation for favor.

PRINCIPLE SEVEN:

SOW FAVOR

The law of sowing and reaping is a God-created spiritual law that works for all the people all the time. For example, the law of gravity works for everyone whether you are a Christian or not. If you throw a ball up in the air, it will come down. God created the law of gravity, and it works! The law of sowing and reaping is the same. Yes, it works… for all the people, all the time.

I have learned in my experience of applying this spiritual law that when I sow favor, I reap it. If you desire to grow in divine favor in your life, then look for people to sow favor into. A farmer who wants a crop of beans will sow bean seeds in proportion to how many beans he wants his field to yield during harvest time. Genesis 8:22 says, "While the earth remains, seedtime and harvest … shall not cease."

What does it look like to sow favor into someone's life? There are many ways you can do this. Even a simple compliment for the way someone ministered, prayed, or even dressed is sowing a seed of favor. Writing a note of encouragement to affirm a person is a seed. Honoring someone is favoring them. Giving a gift to someone is favoring them. Offering an opportunity to an individual is favoring them.

Practice sowing seeds of favor intentionally, and then with the same intention call forth a return of the favor according to God's law of increase. You always reap more than you sow, so beware what you are sowing.

One expression of favor can change a person's life forever. Because you understand divine favor, you can sow God's favor into others generously and see their lives transformed.

This is an awesome way to live! And, the more favor you receive, the more you have to give.

Galatians 6:7

God is not mocked; for whatever a man sows, this he will also reap.

2 Corinthians 9:6

He who sows sparingly will also reap sparingly, and he who sows bountifully will also reap bountifully.

An Activation

Activate the law of sowing and reaping by purposely blessing others with favor. Perhaps make a list of people you would like to sow favor into and think of some creative ways that you can do it (phone call, text, verbal greeting/acknowledgment, card, gift, donation, etc.).

Then believe to reap favor as a result of what you have sown. Your return might not come from those you sowed into, but your seed will produce a crop of favor in your life. Look for it.

> ## To grow in divine favor,
> #### Sow God's favor into others generously
> ##### and see their lives transformed.

PRINCIPLE EIGHT:

OVERCOME RESISTANCE AND ATTACK

Everyone faces challenges in life. Challenges, problems, opposition, and resistance will actually promote you to your next level of success and favor if you embrace them and use them as your stepping stones rather than your stumbling blocks. Your positive perspective is everything.

You are not a victim. You are a victor, and at the end of every trying circumstance, you have the potential to experience new levels of favor that await you.

When you experience resistance, rejection, and maltreatment from others:

- "Humble yourselves under the mighty hand of God, [and believe] that He may exalt you at the proper time" (1 Peter 5:6).

- Examine the opposition and glean from it. Be open to seeing things in your life that need adjustment. "Extract the precious from the worthless ... hold fast to that which is good" (Jeremiah 15:19; 1 Thessalonians 5:21).

- Forgive those who hurt you (see Matthew 6:14).

- "Bless those who curse you, pray for those who mistreat you" (Luke 6:28).

- Wait for the Lord to vindicate. Do not get defensive. "When [your] ways are pleasing to the Lord, He makes even his enemies to be at peace with you" (Proverbs 16:7).

- Stand on the promises of the Lord and decree His favor over your life (see Ephesians 1:3).

- Resist the devil's lies and use your authority in Christ to bind him (see Matthew 16:19).

- Love, Love, Love (see 1 Corinthians 13).

The Lord has called this ministry to the front line. As a forerunner, I am often invited to prophesy and model things that are initially opposed by the body of Christ. During these times, an onlooker might wonder where divine favor is. Some of the opposition has been brutal, and there was not even a hint of favor that manifested in those seasons. When we would humble ourselves, forgive, love, and be teachable, it always increased our favor levels after the season of opposition. I have seen this over and over again.

Everyone faces seasons of resistance and rejection at times when they are doing everything right, but when you humble yourself and trust God's favor in the midst of it, you will come forth with more than you could even ask or think. Jesus was the Champion model for us. He was cruelly rejected and despised by those He came to save, and yet for all eternity He is high and lifted up – He is greatly favored forever!

GOD IS CRAZY IN LOVE WITH YOU.

DRAW NEAR TO HIM AND INTENTIONALLY

RECEIVE FAVOR THROUGH FAITH.

PRINCIPLE NINE:
DRAW NEAR TO GOD

God is not far off, and He has invited us into a close and intimate relationship with Him. Hebrews 4:16 exhorts us to: "Come boldly to the throne of grace, that we may obtain mercy and find grace to help in time of need."

Remember that grace = favor. Grace is God's undeserved, unmerited favor toward you. That favor is your right and your blessing as a child of God. He encourages you through the Word to boldly and confidently approach the throne of grace (favor) to obtain mercy and receive grace (favor).

Your favor comes from God. Draw near to Him and intentionally receive favor through faith. Receive as much as you desire. He is crazy in love with you and wants to reveal His favor.

James 4:7

Resist the devil and he will flee from you. Draw near to God and He will draw near to you.

God is full of love and acceptance toward you. But the devil hates you to the core and wants you to constantly suffer rejection and failure; he wants to conform you to his image – the ultimate failure and eternal rejected one.

The secret to overcoming rejection is to draw near to God. God's presence is a no-go-zone for the devil and when you bask in the fragrance of His love, acceptance, and divine favor toward you, that fragrance gets all over you! All you need is to be in His presence. Remain in His presence and the devil will flee. It is easy!

GOD'S PRESENCE IS A

NO-GO-ZONE FOR THE DEVIL.

BASK IN THE FRAGRANCE OF GOD'S LOVE,

ACCEPTANCE, AND FAVOR.

PRINCIPLE TEN:

FOCUS ON GOD'S GOODNESS

God is good all the time! He is not worried about anything. He is not negative or stressed. He is happy and is always wanting to bless and favor you!

Everyone looks for hope, but often it is lacking. Instead, negativity and pessimism prevail – even in the church! However, favor is all over optimistic people. Why? Because God is optimistic. He always sees the good because He is good.

Romans 8:28:
God causes all things to work together for good to those who love God, to those who are called according to His purpose.

Whatever you focus on, you empower. When you focus on the goodness of God, you will grow in favor with both Him and man.

God loved it when Abraham believed in His goodness and didn't doubt Him. As a result, Abraham was favored – he is even often referred to in the New

Testament. On the other hand, God was saddened by Israel's lack of trust and faith in His goodness and, as a result, they did not enter their promised land.

Your focus on His goodness will create a realm of favor around your life that will follow you all your days.

FAVOR IS YOUR PORTION

You are truly loved and favored by God. He desires you to grow in favor and to enjoy all the benefits of favor for your entire life and throughout all eternity.

Meditate on the principles taught in this book and put into action the things you have learned. They will bring great results for you.

Do not listen to the enemy's lies of rejection, condemnation, and accusation – he would love to conform you to his image, but he is the rejected and condemned one.

You are the highly favored one. That is the truth! Resist the enemy's lies and cleave to the truth all the days of your life.

I am excited for you, my friend. God's divine gift of favor will grant you wonderful blessings in your life.

Let your journey into deeper realms of His outrageous favor and grace begin!

APPENDIX

FAVOR

(from *Decree*, third edition)

In Christ Jesus, I am favored by my heavenly Father. The favor He has given His Son has been given to me. This is undeserved, unmerited favor that is granted me in Christ.

His favor is a free gift to me, for which I am very thankful. As Jesus kept increasing in wisdom and stature, and in favor with God and men, so also do I, because I abide in Jesus and He abides in me.

I embrace the favor of God, for it is better than silver and gold.

The favor of God on my life endures for a lifetime and causes my mountain of influence and blessing to stand strong.

His favor surrounds me like a shield against my enemies.

The Lord favors me with vindication and delights in my prosperity.

His blessing on my life attracts the rich among the people who seek my favor.

By the favor of the Lord, the works of my hands are confirmed and established.

All that I put my hands to is favored. My steps are bathed in butter and the rock pours out oil for me.

As I seek the Lord's favor, He is gracious unto me according to His Word.

I am favored in my home and favored in the workplace. I am favored everywhere I go and in all that I do.

I love wisdom and seek diligently for wisdom and understanding. Therefore I have been granted favor by the Lord and am favored by others.

In the light of my King's face is life, and His favor is like a cloud with the spring rain over me. His favor is like heavenly dew that falls on my life.

I am favored in His presence and He goes before me revealing His goodness and glory to me.

His favor opens doors of opportunity for me that no man can shut.

By His favor I have been granted the keys of the Kingdom and whatever I bind on earth is bound in heaven. Whatever I loose on earth has been loosed in heaven.

His righteous scepter of favor is extended towards me. Whatever I ask in the name of Christ He grants unto me when I make my requests and petitions according to His will.

He daily grants me great favor because of the covenant blood of Christ and the promises in His Word.

Blessed be the Lord who favors His people!

Scriptural References:

Exodus 33:13-19; Esther 5:2; Job 29:6; Psalm 5:12; 30:5,7; 45:6,12; 90:17; 119:58; Proverbs 8:35; 11:27; 16:15; 19:12; 22:1; Isaiah 45:1; Luke 2:52; John 15:7; 17:22

A Friend's Evaluation of
My "First Impression" Dynamics

Dear Friend,

Please answer the following questionnaire openly and honestly. Do not be afraid to give your honest opinion.

1. Overall outward appearance (check all that relate)

___ Well-groomed, neat and tidy

___ Hair is fashionable, well groomed

___ Clothing and accessory styles are becoming and fashionable

___ Footwear is becoming and fashionable

___ Face is groomed well - eyebrows shaped and plucked, makeup applied, facial hair removed (for women); (for men) shaved or groomed beard, unsightly growths removed)

___ Weight is healthy and becoming

___ Fresh breath

___ Fresh body fragrance (i.e., no body odor detected)

___ Teeth are well maintained and white

Share any honest input, comments, or explanations that might help bring awareness to your friend for enhancement of outward appearance.

_____

_____

_____

_____

_____

_____

2. **Countenance** (check all that relate)

___ Optimistic	___ Dancing Eyes
___ Serious	___ Timid
___ Depressed	___ Friendly
___ Boring	___ Joyful
___ Insignificant	

Share any honest input, comments, or explanations that might help bring awareness to your friend regarding the way their countenance is viewed by others.

_____

_____

_____

_____

_____

_____

_____

3. **First impression of personality** (check all that relate)

___ Safe	___ Charismatic
___ Happy/Optimistic	___ Shy
___ Confident	___ Insecure
___ Abrasive	___ Sincere
___ Interested in Others	___ Loving
___ Self-Absorbed	___ Friendly
___ Bold	___ Approachable
___ Feminine	___ Scary
___ Masculine	___ Interesting

___ Disassociated (not focused/mind elsewhere)

Share any honest input, comments, or explanations that might help bring awareness to your friend regarding the way their personality is viewed by others at first impression.

_____

_____

_____

_____

_____

_____

_____

_____

_____

_____

_____

_____

_____

_____

_____

About Patricia King

Patricia King is a respected apostolic minister of the gospel and has been a pioneering voice in ministry, serving for over 30 years as a Christian minister in conference speaking, prophetic service, church leadership, and television and radio appearances. She is the founder of Patricia King Ministries, Women in Ministry Network and Patricia King Institute, the co-founder of XPmedia.com, and director of Women on the Frontlines. She has written many books, produced numerous CDs and DVDs, and hosts her TV program, *Patricia King – Everlasting Love TV*. She is also a successful business owner and an inventive entrepreneur. Patricia's reputation in the Christian community is world-renowned.

To Connect:

Patricia King website: PatriciaKing.com

Facebook: Facebook.com/PatriciaKingPage

Patricia King Institute: PatriciaKingInstitute.com

Women on the Frontlines and Women in Ministry Network: Woflglobal.com

Patricia King – Everlasting Love TV show and many other video teachings by Patricia: XPmedia.com

Receive a Glorious Revelation

Discover a path of miracle replenishment and increase in everything that pertains to you – your physical strength, your love, your time, your provision, your gifts, your anointing, and anything else that flows from you to God and others.

Receive this God-given revelation through biblical examples, insights and keys, along with practical applications, personal testimonies, and decrees for activation.

Experience Financial Breakthrough

You were created to know abundance and blessing. Not only is God well able to prosper His people, but He has given us the tools to lay hold of abundance right now. Patricia opens your eyes to God's prosperity plan for you and gives you powerful Scripture-based decrees to open heaven's windows of blessing over your life.

The Word of God never returns void; it always produces fruit. Grab hold of these decrees and get your financial breakthrough!

Additional copies of this book and other
book titles from Patricia King are available at:

Amazon.com
PatriciaKing.com

Bulk/wholesale prices for stores and ministries:

Please contact: resource@patriciaking.com

Patricia King Enterprises